# HASTINGS
## IN OLD PHOTOGRAPHS
### A SECOND SELECTION

A NEW TRAM sparkles in the morning sunlight in 1905 at the Memorial in the town centre. With their yellow and brown livery, trams were an exciting sight, and soon replaced horse buses.

# HASTINGS
## IN OLD PHOTOGRAPHS
### A SECOND SELECTION

COLLECTED BY
## PAMELA HAINES

Alan Sutton Publishing Limited
Phoenix Mill · Far Thrupp · Stroud · Gloucestershire

First Published 1991

**British Library Cataloguing in Publication Data**

Hastings in old photographs: a second selection.
I. Haines, Pamela, *1935*–
942.259

ISBN 0-86299-863-8

DEDICATION: To Gavin S. Haines and Kean D. Haines – Hastingers both.

Typeset in 9/10 Korinna.
Typesetting and origination by
Alan Sutton Publishing Limited.
Printed in Great Britain by
The Bath Press, Avon.

# CONTENTS

# INTRODUCTION

This second selection of old photographs covers the history of Hastings from about 1900 to 1950. It not only fills in some of the inevitable gaps in the first selection but enables us to understand the town's later development more clearly.

There can be no better start to this understanding than by examining the photograph on the cover of this book, which must be the most dramatic photograph ever taken of Hastings. The date is March 1943. German fighter-bombers are attacking the town in a daytime raid. They have flown in at such a low altitude from over the sea that anti-aircraft gunners at Hastings Castle are unable to line them up in their sights.

This was history still being made at William the Conqueror's first English castle. Built after 1066, its ruins still dominate the modern town; but it was never actually used against a foreign enemy until the Second World War. Having myself witnessed a similar air-raid from the nearby East Hill, I can vouch for the accuracy of the photograph and the perilous atmosphere it captures. The photographer, Haywood McGee, sold the picture to the famous magazine *Picture Post* but it was not published because of its obvious value to the enemy.

The Second World War represents the last great peak of danger and resolve in any British town's history. But Hastings, like any other town, had its own reasons for being affected in its own particular way by the last war. These reasons can be poignantly understood if we study the whole range of photographs and 'get the feel' of them. The town has had a bad time over the years. Its failure to prosper along the lines of other resorts has often baffled many a resident, but there have always been citizens who have loved the town. Their local patriotism comes across in many contemporary publications. Notably, in *The Memoirs of a Mayor of Hastings*, the then mayor, Alderman Dymond, recovering from the excitement of the visit by the then Prince of Wales, writes lyrically of his vision of Hastings as a future 'garden city'. As early as 1880, a group of local residents and businessmen had already combined to form the Borough Association. Their aim was to promote the town not only as a seaside resort, but as a wonderful place to live. Through their personal subscriptions, they published the first illustrated town guides in the form we know them today and employed the best photographers whose work we see in this book.

The promotion of Hastings for seaside holidaymaking was of great benefit to the town. Many residents were able to survive the bad times of the Edwardian period by letting lodgings – in much the same way, in today's recession, as they board foreign students. During the First World War, many residents accommodated the troops billeted in the town, but holidaymakers still came.

By the early 1920s, the Borough Association had a new secretary – a returned army officer, W.H. Dyer. The Town Council soon took it over, with its secretary, in the newly formed Publicity Department. Bill Dyer's energy and enthusiasm became the driving force behind all the subsequent official publicity, but he was ably assisted by Bill Vint. At the same time, the 'Souvenir Normand' (founded locally in the 1880s) was revived. Formed to promote local connections with Normandy, it was the origin of modern efforts to promote the '1066 country' as a publicity theme. Significantly, you can find Bill Dyer in the photograph on p. 90 – dressed as William the Conqueror.

Another big driving force was the Borough Engineer, Sidney Little. He was responsible for the developments to be seen in other photographs – such as the open-air bathing-pool at Grosvenor Gardens and the massive remodelling of the sea front. He was known locally as 'the concrete king' because of the staggering amount of concrete which his constructions demanded.

Important, but less dramatic, changes had by this time already taken place. The Infirmary, featured on earlier postcards, had been replaced by the White Rock Pavilion, the Royal East Sussex Hospital had been opened, and the Museum had been moved from the Brassey Institute in Claremont to the attractive building at John's Place in Cambridge Road. The town had by this time also decided to have a proper public library in the old Brassey Institute. (Lord Brassey had given the town both the building and a lot of his own books.) Despite the town's problem in still having a large number of unemployed residents in the 1920s, all this development was a big step towards improving the town for residents and visitors alike. The stage was well set for even better things, and the town felt justifiably proud of the royal visit in 1927.

Examining the photographs of this visit today, it is sad to think how soon yet another slump was to impair the town's progress – to say nothing of the looming shadow of another war. Yet most townspeople remained indomitable. Many volunteered for training in civil defence, the Auxiliary Fire Service and the Special Constabulary. In these more cynical days it is both touching and thrilling to examine photographs of their parades.

After the Second World War there was a revival of local optimism. A spirit similar to that of the 1920s motivated a new set of plans. But any progress was to be an uphill struggle. Apart from war damage, many buildings had been unoccupied for years and had deteriorated beyond repair. Even the St Leonards Pier (which is featured so grandly in this book) had become an abandoned skeleton. Its owners had mysteriously disappeared and the Local Authority had to pay for the demolition.

With this general impression in mind, each individual photograph becomes even more poignant and fascinating if you examine it with a magnifying glass. Many of those I have chosen from the 1900s are old picture postcards, but they are remarkable (when you compare them with present day postcards) for being such a candid record of ordinary people and events. The old photographers didn't stick to conventional views of the castle and the sea front. They went 'behind the scenes' into the quieter streets and roads to take what are today known as 'genre' and 'documentary' photographs. (A 'genre' photograph tends to be more posed than a so-called 'documentary' photograph.) Despite being in monochrome, their work was directly influenced by the art of watercolour and oil painting. Some photographers were in fact skilled painters – Fred Judge being the most notable local exemplar – but all have given us a treasure trove of detail within a properly composed frame.

Some of the photographs have more 'anecdotal' details than others. In other words, they 'tell us a story' about the people whom the photographer has caught at a certain moment in time. The story is limited, of course, to a simple human action – such as the lady fumbling anxiously in her handbag before boarding a tram.

Then you detect the conductor's impatient hand upon the bell as he gazes upon her from his platform, and the whole scene springs to life as a dramatic study. Sometimes the people in a photograph are more enigmatic and can become strangely haunting when you visit the same scene yourself.

A final point to bear in mind when studying the actual people in old photographs of Hastings – many of the them are very well dressed. But they are not necessarily people of leisure. Many were railway day-trippers in their Sunday best. It was also the custom for local residents to dress in their finery for a weekend stroll along the sea front. At Easter and Whitsun the essential requirement for ladies was a new or retrimmed hat. Such apparent extravagance can be misleading. It often conceals what must have been a hard life.

Lastly, it is the history of the photographs themselves (as distinct from the history of the town) which makes the study of old photographs so completely fascinating. Obviously this fascination relates mostly to the lives of the photographers and the way they did their work. Fred Judge we have already mentioned, but it is Frederick Nutt Broderick (1854-1913) whom I have mostly relied upon to illustrate the Edwardian period. He operated from Ryde, Isle of Wight, and started by going into business with his father (a printer and engraver) in 1878. He produced prints and stereoscopic lantern slides before venturing into the expanding postcard trade. We can picture him working his way along the south coast with his eldest daughter, Aurora, as his assistant. Possibly his wife and his other daughter accompanied him, but we do know (from studying an informal family group which he probably took by remote control – p. 85) that Aurora appears in some of his Hastings postcards. She appears to be a sort of good luck charm which it is amusing, for us, to identify. (He named the series of postcards I have used the 'Aurora' series – this designation being printed in the stamp space.) His work has a special charm, much of it 'anecdotal', and it is interesting to compare it with some almost identical shots by the French photographer Louis Levy ('L.L.').

Old photographs of every kind are often overlooked as source material for local history. When assembled in either thematic or chronological order, they suggest ideas for very detailed research. In particular, enlarged copies reveal previously unseen aspects of social history – such as people trying, in their different ways, to earn money on the sea front. Architectural details are important clues to periods of growth or decline. In these photographs of Hastings, we can see that the town has sometimes competed with other resorts to the detriment of its own fine architectural heritage. In 1933, for example, Bexhill opened its splendidly modern De La Warr Pavilion. Not to be outdone, Hastings produced Marine Court five years later – with its big restaurants, its shops and its flats. Could this really be said to be an improvement upon James Burton's architecture?

Approaching the end of the second half of the twentieth century, it is indeed thought-provoking to study the first half through these old photographs.

# The Old Town

ALL SAINTS' CHURCH (once All Hallows') was built in the early fifteenth century. It had been moved from a site closer to the sea. Next to the Georgian rectory are the stables, still partly in use as a private garage. Because the church appears in so many picturesque old views it is a good focal point for a walk around the Old Town. (Blomfield, 1910)

ALL SAINTS' STREET in 1910, taken from the high pavement opposite. On the left, No. 125, 'Shovell's' (c. 1450–80), was once two houses.

THE CINQUE PORTS ARMS, All Saints' Street, 1930s. Named in 1842, this pub was on the site of the Chequer Inn of 1642. Examine the next door cottage on its left before looking at the next photograph.

FOR A SHORT PERIOD BEFORE AND AFTER THE SECOND WORLD WAR it became fashionable to re-create 'Tudor' houses. The Cinque Ports Arms and its neighbours on each side are known to have stood on the site of three Georgian houses.

11

AT THE SEA END of All Saints' Street, early 1900s, before the restoration shown below.

SYMPATHETICALLY RESTORED in the 1930s, these houses date from about 1450.

THE SEA END of All Saints' Street in 1939. The shop fronts indicate a conversion from timber framing. No. 70 was part of a Wealden hall house and has now been restored. It shows how timber framing had become unpopular and houses of this type had been disguised.

THE SAME UNKNOWN PHOTOGRAPHER has noted on the back of each print that he used a Leica camera. A quiet and closer view.

ALL SAINTS' STREET, 1945, showing the lapse from the quietly picturesque into the grim deterioration after the Second World War. (Compare with the previous two photographs.)

ALL SAINTS' STREET, First World War. A final look back from the top of the street. Now it is difficult to visualize its complicated building history. The original fine timber-framed street was altered by owners responding to building fashions. Some rebuilt, but the less well-off plastered over the timber-framed facades.

THE FOLLOWING FOUR PHOTOGRAPHS show the cottages which had been built in the long gardens of All Saints' Street during the nineteenth-century increase in population. This shows Providence Row, built in 1835 in the garden of No. 131 All Saints' Street.

THIS ROW OF COTTAGES was called the Creek after a small inlet from the sea that had been filled in near Courthouse Street.

UNION ROW, 1930s. These cottages began at No. 129 All Saints' Street.

WATERLOO PLACE was once called the Upper Lane where there was a bridge over the Bourne stream. It was renamed in 1815 after the battle. These cottages and all those in the previous three photographs were demolished before the Second World War to make way for the eventual through road known as The Bourne (the A259).

A PANORAMA OF THE OLD TOWN FROM THE EAST HILL. Standing at this viewpoint today, you can see how the Old Town has been cut in half by The Bourne. The steps (extreme left) were originally built for the use of the workmen building the East Hill cliff railway in 1902. (Broderick, 1905)

AN AMUSING SHOT OF HASTINGS FISHERMEN about to be taken to vote for the Conservative candidate, Harvey Du Cros, in 1906. In the back row are Richard, James and Edward Adams. A smiling Mr Robert Adams is in the bowler, seated. Some must have had to stand on the running-board.

THE ENTRANCE TO ALL SAINTS' STREET FROM THE SEA END. The brick facade behind Pleasant Row (left), which was then a grocer's, was 'Tudorized' after the Second World War and became 'Pulpit Gate'. (Blomfield, 1930s)

THE LONG GONE MERCER'S BANK opposite Pleasant Row, about 1900. It is now Winkle Island.

THE BOURNE about 1950. The King's Head, on the corner of Courthouse Street, stands on the site of a much earlier inn, The George. The fine timber-framed house on the left (No. 29 The Bourne) has a late fifteenth-century date. Originally it faced onto a little square on the Courthouse Street side. Surprisingly, the house next door (left) has been found to be older. In addition, archaeologists working on the old Phoenix Brewery site (now Bourne Court) found pottery dating from around the time of the Norman Conquest.

THE FISHERMEN'S WELCOME ARCH, August 1900, designed to welcome Lord Brassey on his return from Australia. He had been Governor of Victoria for five years, and could always be relied upon to give financial help to distressed fishermen.

AN UNKNOWN BAND is enthusiastically playing on the beach to the east of the lifeboat house in the early 1900s. Curiously, the audience is on a platform (in the background) while the performers are seated on wooden crates.

THIS VIEW OF THE EAST HILL CLIFF RAILWAY UNDER CONSTRUCTION reflects Broderick's keen interest in people of all classes. This small family look like day trippers. (Broderick, 1902)

THE VICTORIAN LIFEBOAT HOUSE (the tower), which opened in 1882 and was demolished in 1959, is visible in both photographs. (Broderick, 1905)

EAST PARADE, 1900. These neat and doll-like houses facing the sea vary in date from about 1790 to the early 1900s. They epitomize seaside charm and elegance, but, as lodging houses, they were hard work to run.

EAST PARADE, 1913. Postcards of storm damage were very popular, like this one of 'a memorable Easter gale.'

THE HIGH STREET in about 1930. Can you spot the fascia for Hart's and find the exact position from which this photograph was taken? You can still buy your kippers from this well-known Old Town shop, but you'll be baffled until you realize that the photograph shows it on the opposite side of the road. It moved to its present-day site (No. 71) after being bombed in the Second World War. (Blomfield)

THE CIVIC CHURCH PARADE on 15 January 1936, being led into St Clement's church by the Chief Constable, Supt Buddle (behind the sergeant, centre), followed by the town crier. The mayor, Arthur Blackman, is between the two mace-bearers. The guard of honour is being formed by the St John Ambulance Brigade.

A WIDER AND CLOSER VIEW OF THE SHOPS AND HOUSES which are detectable in the previous photograph. A young lady is perilously cleaning an upstairs window above Judge's ('the Old Cake and Bun Shop') on the left of Warner's. The photograph is from about 1930.

THE ROEBUCK INN (now the Roebuck Surgery and Roebuck Street). Can you detect the outline of a roebuck above the sign over the errand boy's bicycle? This old timber-framed inn had its beams plastered over. (Blomfield, 1930)

THIS VIEW, looking up the High Street, shows the increasing effects of traffic congestion in the 1930s which eventually led to the construction of The Bourne as the major through road.

AN UNDATED PHOTOGRAPH OF THE SWAN INN which stood on the corner of the High Street, opposite St Clement's church. The hub of social life in the Old Town, it was always busy with meetings, large dinners, assemblies and balls. A famous coaching inn, it had extensive stabling behind, entered by an archway from the High Street. The site is first mentioned in 1523 as Le Swane. This picture shows the Victorian rebuild of 1879.

LOOKING DOWN THE HIGH STREET towards The Swan at the far end on the right. The clock on the old town hall (right) can still be seen. It is now an interesting Museum of Local History. (Blomfield, 1930)

THE TRAGIC END OF THE SWAN on 23 May 1943. It was bombed one Sunday lunchtime and many people died. Never rebuilt, a garden of remembrance commemorates the site of an inn with over four hundred years of history.

FIGGETT'S, THE ANTIQUE DEALERS, at 42a High Street, on the corner of Courthouse Street. This shop is still recognizable today as the lapidary selling all manner of fascinating stones. The roof is late fifteenth century. (Blomfield, 1930)

THE BOMB DAMAGE TO FIGGETT'S and other properties, such as Reeve's and Hart's, all happened on the same day as the total destruction of The Swan – 23 May 1943. Medieval cellars were found on this corner after the clear-up, with burn marks from fourteenth-century raids by the French.

THESE GEORGIAN STABLES (built between 1739 and 1746 for Old Hastings House) looked like this for many years until converted into today's Stables Theatre which opened in 1959.

AT THE TOP OF HIGH STREET is this famous old cottage, wrongly known as the home of Titus Oates. The real one was a little further south and no longer exists. Here, the cottage is being repaired after bombing in 1942.

CROFT ROAD, 1932. Despite the added railings and other changes, this road still retains the same air of exclusivity — always attractive to visitors wandering up towards the Georgian splendours of The Croft.

CROFT CHAPEL. This fine brick building at the entrance to Croft Road was pulled down for flats in 1972. Long disused, it had at one time been used as a film studio by George Ivan Barnett, the local film maker and photographer. (J.M. Baines, 1972)

THE HASTINGS LIFEBOAT, THE *CYRIL AND LILIAN BISHOP*, used as a pulpit for Blessing the Sea, the fishing community's equivalent of Harvest Festival, during the 1930s.

FIELD MARSHAL MONTGOMERY IS MADE A MEMBER OF THE WINKLE CLUB on board the *Cyril and Lilian Bishop* at Winkle Island in 1946. From left to right; William Martin (Coxswain), William Muggeridge, Harry Muggeridge, Monty, Bunk Harffey (Hon. Sec.), Frank Edmunds, Mayor F.W. Chambers, Bert White (between mayor and mace-bearer).

A WET DAY FOR THE SPECIAL CONSTABLES parading on the sea front on 23 April 1939, with East Cliff House in the background. The specials had been trained in air-raid precautions from 1936 onwards. The Commandant H.A. Shirley is facing the camera, his gloved hands in a curious thumb-twiddling position. One of the specials seems to be having a good sneeze.

# Ore Village and the Country Park

WALKING HOME UP FAIRLIGHT ROAD. The mother pushing the pram wears a stylish flat hat and well-fitted jacket. The older lady, possibly grandmama, has an old-fashioned bonnet.

A 1905 POSTCARD made from Broderick's previous photograph.

OLD LONDON ROAD. Fairlight Road (in the previous two photographs) is up to the right past The Cabin. (Broderick, 1905)

OLD LONDON ROAD, ORE, looking towards the gates of the Fairlight Sanitorium (now Barrington House). The Rye Road had not yet been cut through. (Broderick, 1905)

LIFE IN ORE VILLAGE was so quiet, it would seem, that Broderick has had to be content with a plain statement, or a general view, of Old London Road in the opposite direction. (Broderick, 1905)

EVEN IF YOU ARE A LOCAL MOTORIST who passes through this junction every day, you might find this old photograph of Old London Road hard to identify. The Royal Sussex Arms, although long since rebuilt, should give you an important clue. If you now 'remove' Dawes Drug Stores from the picture (as it was removed for widening the road for the trams in 1905), you will recognize Frederick Road leading to St Helen's Hospital. The old boundary stone between Hastings and Ore is still to be found if you go looking for it. (Ask older residents to identify the position of the former Dolls' Hospital before you go searching.) Is the term 'drug stores' an example of an early Americanism in Hastings? This photograph, we may presume, was taken just before the pub was due to open. (Even the dog reclining at the door is waiting patiently.)

WARREN GLEN, FAIRLIGHT has always been beautiful, but this appears to be an Edwardian attempt to 'pep up' a dull view with a superimposed theatrical couple.

LOVERS' SEAT, AT FAIRLIGHT, 1910, with such well-made steps but an astonishingly neglected fence. The dandified lover, with his buttonhole and far too slender a cane for such a rough walk, appears to have an enormous right hand.

LOVERS' SEAT in the 1930s. A publicity photograph to compare with the previous example. Although the people are more relaxed and informal, three of them seem to be posing in a foolhardy position.

A FORLORN AND LONELY GENTLEMAN GAZING INTO THE SEA while the sturdy Lovers' Seat remains sadly empty. To judge from the Edwardian golfing-suit, we can assume that the photographer induced a golfer (from the nearby course) to pose. Perhaps this was designed for a 'wish-you-were-here' postcard.

THESE COASTGUARD COTTAGES IN ECCLESBOURNE GLEN were to disappear into the sea by 1961. (Broderick, 1905)

ALL SOULS' CHURCH from Edmund Road, Clive Vale. Designed by Sir Arthur Blomfield, this was the last Victorian parish church built in Hastings (in 1891). 'Clive Vale' means 'the valley of the cliffs'. (Broderick, 1905)

A MEMBER OF THE WOMEN'S VOLUNTARY POLICE SERVICE during the First World War, at the dog pound. Women were not officially recognized as police officers until after the war, Hastings having its first official WPC in 1937. The pound was at the base of the East Hill Cliffs at Rock-a-Nore.

# Royal Visit, 1927

HASTINGS WAS HOST TO HRH THE PRINCE OF WALES (later Edward VIII) on 6 April 1927. This photograph shows him on the lifeboat at the Old Town – a happy and informal moment of the kind he most enjoyed.

THE OFFICIAL OPENING OF THE WHITE ROCK PAVILION. The prince seems almost intimidated by his own popularity as he addresses the huge crowd. Behind him and in front of the gentlemen of the press, are (from left to right): Mr Norman Gray, Alderman George Cox, Captain Bruce Ogilvie, His Worship the Mayor (T.H. Dymond) and Mr D.V. Jackson, the Town Clerk.

YOU SHOULD HAVE NO DIFFICULTY in discerning the rather isolated figure of HRH striding away from the Pavilion, the pace being set by the chief constable.

ONCE AROUND THE CORNER, a fairly stiff climb now followed for HRH up the steps to the White Rock Gardens. Here, 6,000 schoolchildren awaited him.

AN ENORMOUS BEVY OF NURSES (which must have gladdened his heart) is waving goodbye after the prince's brief visit to the Royal East Sussex Hospital. It was opened in 1923 and is due to be replaced by the Conquest Hospital on the Ridge.

AT DENMARK PLACE with the Mayor T.H. Dymond, leaving the Queen's Hotel after lunch. The crowded balcony of the hotel in the background has now been converted into a restaurant.

CAROLINE PLACE. Before the march-past of the ex-servicemen, the prince greets their disabled comrades. The wicker bath-chairs seem poignantly old-fashioned, even for 1927. Behind the prince is Major-General Sir Owen Lloyd VC.

THE PRINCE REVIEWING VETERANS of the Boer War and the First World War. He is standing almost opposite Pelham Crescent.

HRH ALIGHTS AT THE FISHMARKET to a formal cheer from fishermen in newly polished boots, but he and the fishermen were soon completely at ease with one another.

HRH CLAMBERS ABOARD A LIFEBOAT, the *Charles Arkoll 2*. He doesn't know it, but he is shortly to be presented with a gold winkle by the Winkle Club – always a happy surprise for distinguished visitors.

THE PRINCE IN CONVERSATION WITH Mr Henry Samson JP, Hon. Sec. of the local RNLI (second from right).

HRH MEETS VARIOUS MEMBERS OF THE CREW. The steadfastly upraised oars are a mark of respect on this lifeboat without an engine. It was in service from 1901 to 1931.

A GROUP OF WINKLE CLUB MEMBERS after HRH's unscheduled initiation on the lifeboat. In the centre is Councillor Stevens, and behind him (pipe between his teeth) is Lord Eustace Percy, the MP for Hastings.

THE FISHERMEN'S TRADITIONAL ARCH OF WELCOME incorporated spectacular fish neatly entombed in ice blocks.

AFTER VISITING THE BUCHANAN HOSPITAL, the prince takes his leave of Dr F. Shaw and others, including a huddled snapshotter (right).

THE SECRETARY TO THE HOSPITAL, Mr Guy Henderson, displaying the prince's autographed portrait after the departure. Mr A.D. Snow and Dr Shaw are on his left, and the matron (Miss E. Webb) and Phyllis Moyce (who presented the bouquet) are on his right.

ORE VILLAGE. Here the prince stopped to lay a wreath on the war memorial at Christ church.

AT FAIRLIGHT Councillor F.W. Morgan is telling a now rather tired HRH all about the town's recent purchase of the Firehills as a public open space.

THIS SHOT OF THE ROYAL MOTOR IN QUEEN'S ROAD (today opposite Ward's, the outfitters) will remind many older people of their most lasting impression of the visit. For them, the image that stays in the mind is that of the silver Rolls – like a silver coach containing this almost magically popular prince.

# SECTION FOUR

# Central Hastings

THESE WELL-OFF MEMBERS OF THE COMMUNITY are strolling along Caroline Place in quite heavy clothes. Yet it must have been quite a mild day, early as the season was, because a distant lady is even sheltering under a sunshade. (Broderick, 1905)

A PHOTOGRAPHER PHOTOGRAPHED. A tripod has been set up to 'take' the little girl and the group around the rowing-boat on the right. In the foreground, two boatmen are looking for last minute customers to fill the spaces in the pleasure yacht. (Broderick, 1905)

UNDER THE SEA-WALL, OPPOSITE THE QUEEN'S HOTEL. Probably taken in 1900, it is a valuable shot of much older equipment in action. An assistant is holding up a sun-shield while a female assistant is attracting the children. The photographer is about to use his bowler for covering the lens.

JUST OPPOSITE THE QUEEN'S HOTEL, the *New Albertine* awaits more customers before setting off. Built in 1891, she was the largest pleasure yacht working the beach and remained in service until 1924. A boy pushing a bicycle near the water's edge provides a curious touch. (Broderick, 1905)

A SUBDUED PARTY RETURNING FROM A PLEASURE TRIP. Despite their nostalgic appearance, these boats were notorious for sea-sickness, and having no lifebelts they would not be allowed to sail today.

AN AERIAL VIEW OF THE VICTORIAN TOWN CENTRE, taken from 800 ft in 1919. On the beach the *New Albertine* pleasure yacht is drawn up near the mouth of the Priory stream culvert.

RIDING IN A WAGGONETTE, Edwardian visitors enjoy a 'round the town' ride. This four-horse equipage is making its stately progress past the Albert Memorial – the Clock Tower, familiar for so many years until its removal in 1973.

AT THE MEMORIAL, 24 June 1902, with the old post office in the background. You can work out where the newspaper seller is standing if you visit the much changed scene. His placard reads 'The Coronation – Alarming News'. (The coronation of Edward VII had to be postponed because of his operation for appendicitis.) The boy in knickerbockers is more interested in the camera than the alarming news.

THE MELODIOUS CHIMES OF THE ALBERT MEMORIAL CLOCK TOWER could be heard over a large part of the town. Built in 1863 after the death of Queen Victoria's husband, it was a popular meeting place. Behind it is The York, a Victorian pub closed in 1965 and since demolished. Although it looked like this for many years, this photograph was taken in the early 1900s.

THE TOWN CENTRE (The Memorial). The tram, No. 28, is *en route* to the cemetery via Queen's Road. The waiting carriage (right) is a Victoria, used in summer by well-to-do ladies. (Broderick, 1905)

ALMOST THE SAME VIEWPOINT TWENTY YEARS LATER. There is still the same enviable freedom to wander all over the road, but changes are in the offing. The ladies' clothing is much more relaxed and would not be unacceptable today. The facade of Plummer Roddis (now Debenham's) was to be remodelled later, in 1927.

AN EASILY RECOGNIZED CORNER OF WELLINGTON SQUARE. This photograph, taken in the 1900s, leaves us with a haunting image of a strange lady (right). She is teetering towards the kerb – perhaps to cross the road. The lady on her left looks quizzical and even rather startled, but perhaps she is a companion rather than a separate pedestrian.

VESTIGES OF THE FASHIONABLE LIFE were still clinging to Wellington Square in 1905. In the 1820s and '30s it had been a focal point for some of the most dashing members of high society, who would rent houses for the season.

THESE REGENCY COTTAGES with their exquisite porches and bow windows were in Castle Hill Road. They were demolished in the 1960s and a private car park now occupies a part of the site.

THIS PART OF THE PARADE was opposite the now demolished Beach Terrace. The entrance to Pelham Street (now Woolworth's) was just behind the lovely gas lamp. The smiling girl nearest to us at the rail is probably the photographer's daughter. (Broderick, 1905)

THIS WIDER VIEW OF THE PHOTOGRAPH on p. 53 reveals more of Broderick's photographic humour. The two boatmen are waiting for clients, but their hopeful anticipation is being met with disdain by the two ladies in their furs. The disdain, in part, is being returned: one boatman remains truculently seated and the other keeps his hands in his pockets. (Broderick, 1905)

A JAM-PACKED CROWD for yet another new bandstand. This one was at Caroline Place – eventually re-sited to avoid the south-west winds. (Broderick, 1905)

THE ROYAL OAK HOTEL IN CAROLINE PLACE was a very popular commercial hotel built about 1825. The clock on the left hand side advertises a dry cleaners in the basement. The hotel was bombed in 1943. (Broderick, 1905)

A LIVELY SCENE AT DENMARK PLACE featuring street hawkers, children enjoying donkey rides and a capstan for the pleasure yachts. Readers of Robert Tressell will notice that Gatti's Restaurant (left) catered for 'beanfeasts'. (Broderick, 1905)

THE PHOTOGRAPHER'S DAUGHTER is posing (left of centre) almost opposite Denmark Place. Sadly, the Queen's Hotel (but without the cupolas) is the only surviving building in this scene. (Broderick, 1905)

THE LONG WOODEN SEAT IN FRONT OF ROBERTSON TERRACE. The grand old railings went for scrap in the Second World War. The sailor-suited boy is crossing the road so fast his leg is blurred. Is he returning from the beach to his snoozing parents, and what is he carrying? Could it be a diabolo, or a bat and ball? (Broderick, 1905)

CARLISLE PARADE. On the left, by the railing, a girl of about twenty walks towards us. She is Broderick's daughter who carries a photographer's case of the period. (Broderick, 1905)

PARADE. HASTINGS.

AN ENLARGED POSTCARD OF CARLISLE PARADE yields much 'anecdotal' material. The bootblack and the goat-cart proprietor (in front of the 'modern' motor car) have yet to attract any

custom. Was this taken after lunch when holidaymakers were relatively torpid? (Broderick, 1905)

THIS CLOSER VIEW OF CARLISLE PARADE is a more modern photograph than the previous one. It shows one of the best surviving examples of Victorian architecture in Hastings, built in 1851. The architect, A.J. Humbert, was a favourite of Albert, the Prince Consort, who employed him to redesign Sandringham. He was also used by Queen Victoria to design Albert's Mausoleum at Frognal.

CARLISLE PARADE, looking eastwards. The ladies are wearing remarkably beautiful clothes for the beach. The tethered beach-horse must have found the heat unbearable under the sun-trapping wall. As today, the men on the left are craning their necks to look at the ladies below – hoping, in those days, to glimpse a bare ankle? (Broderick, 1905)

THE TRAM ENTERING ROBERTSON STREET has stopped for a solitary lady, but the conductor's impatient hand is already on the bell and the lady is fumbling in her bag for the fare before she boards. (Broderick, 1907)

THIS PHOTOGRAPH is taken from much the same position as the previous view but at a wider angle to show Carlisle Parade. It is obviously taken before the trams arrived – compare with the enlargement on pp. 68-69. (Broderick, 1905)

A CHARMINGLY AMATEUR SNAPSHOT of an Edwardian lady with the Hastings pier behind her. The big hat must have been well anchored with hat-pins in the obvious breeze.

FASHION BECAME MORE CASUAL in 1912, and Gladys Watson (later Mrs Long) is dressed in the latest mode: a long narrow skirt and relaxed neckline. A great change from the tight corsets and high stiff necks of earlier years – especially for strolling on the sea front by Caroline Place!

OPPOSITE THE CORNER OF WHITE ROCK AND ROBERTSON STREET a goat-cart awaits its young customers. Donkey rides and goat-carting were very popular with young visitors.

TO JUDGE FROM HIS BEARING, this is probably an ex-serviceman playing in the gutter opposite Robertson Terrace (about 1900). He is blind (his stick hangs from his neck) and he has provided his well-behaved dog with a piece of matting.

THE BANDSTAND AT WHITE ROCK which was erected in 1895. Broderick often prefers to have people facing or walking towards his camera. The two private nurses beside the bath-chairs were probably asked to pose. Compare this with the same view below. (Broderick, 1905)

17 HASTINGS. — The Parade — LL.

THE PHOTOGRAPHER 'L.L.' characteristically prefers shots of people looking or moving away from the camera, and he obtains a 'continental' effect which differs from the very English Broderick. The white footing for the title adds an extra touch of glamour. (Louis Levy)

THE SAME BANDSTAND from another angle. Again, most people are moving towards the camera. (Broderick, 1905)

COMPARE THIS 'L.L.' WITH THE PREVIOUS PHOTOGRAPH. Various details show the difference of a few years, but 'L.L.' has moved forward – you can work out his tripod position from the Broderick photograph. (Louis Levy)

WHITE ROCK. Various details, such as the absence of trams, show this photograph was taken before 1907. The bonnet of the old lady (left) was already old-fashioned while the distant lady with the muff and the energetically chatting lady in the foreground are bang up to date with feathers, and even whole stuffed birds, adorning their hats. (Broderick)

ALMOST THE SAME SCENE. In the distance, beyond the bandstand, is the part of the sea front then known as 'Splash Point'. Despite the later widening of the promenade, stormy seas still break over the wall and the name seems worthy of revival.

THE PROMENADE, about 1910. An Edwardian lady is walking so briskly that she has to clutch her hat. The gentleman with the sailor-suited offspring seems much more leisurely. A happy photograph, but, as always, one wonders at the war time grief which 1914 was to bring into these people's lives.

THIS POSTCARD of 1922 shows the same bandstand, but it has been moved nearer the pier and is being used as a temporary war memorial. A nurse is collecting for the War Memorial Fund. Returning servicemen wanted the fund to benefit the living, and so the fund helped both the Buchanan and the Royal East Sussex hospitals a few years later.

HASTINGS RAILWAY STATION in the 1900s. Now completely remodelled, it looked very similar to Warrior Square Station. Can you detect the line-up of haulage vans and the triple gas lamps in the centre of the flowerbed which two gardeners are busily watering?

GLYNE GAP RAILWAY STATION between West St Leonards and Bexhill. It briefly served the nearby gasworks (1905-1915) and was a boon to visitors making for the uncrowded beach.

QUEEN'S ROAD. The enormous porch is the entry to the General Post Office (built 1869, moved to Cambridge Road in 1930). The ladies' skirts must have got filthy after trailing across roads like this. (Broderick, 1905)

EMPIRE (NOW COMMONWEALTH) DAY CELEBRATIONS on 24 May 1912. The police contingent is passing The Pilot at the junction of Stone Street and Queen's Road. This pub was later converted into a shop.

THE CINQUE PORTS RVC (Rifle Volunteer Corps) in the forecourt of Hastings station. Their uniforms were scarlet, with blue facings. The time is about 1900.

A CYCLE PLATOON OF THE RVC, also in the forecourt of Hastings station.

BANDSMEN OF THE RIFLE VOLUNTEER CORPS on the same occasion.

THE 1ST SUSSEX REV (Royal Engineer Volunteers) practice bridge building in Alexandra Park. This photograph is also thought to be about 1900.

THE SOUVENIR NORMAND, entertained in Alexandra Park in 1903, are listening to the opera *Les Cloches de Corneville* (The Chimes of Normandy). The large orchestra and painted classical proscenium show the degree of effort put into such events.

FRENCH LADIES OF THE SOUVENIR NORMAND in 1903 are thoughtfully inspecting the ruins of William the Conqueror's castle at Hastings. Very dressed up for this visit, the most ornate lady has a reticule at her waist.

FOOTBALL AT THE CRICKET GROUND in 1906, with Hastings United playing Rock-a-Nore. Enthusiasts may care to work out the action prior to the shutter click. (The goalie seems very confused.) Mr Victor Vidler is second right.

DEVONSHIRE ROAD. A late Victorian terrace with the added bonus of a grandstand view of the cricket ground from the back. This must have made them very prosperous small hotels and lodging houses during the great days of cricket at Hastings. (Broderick, 1905)

MILWARD ROAD, taken when Robert Tressell was living in the top flat of the tallest house on the left. There is still a newsagent opposite where he used to buy his cigarettes, writing materials, etc. (Broderick, 1905)

MOUNT PLEASANT ROAD, named after an eighteenth-century house, rebuilt by a London brewer in 1828 and sold for development in 1894. It stood in the centre of the terrace (right). The Congregational church has been demolished. (Broderick, 1905)

MANY OF THE EARLY POSTCARDS reproduced in this book were taken by the photographer, Frederick Nutt Broderick. He is seen here with his wife Emily (right) and daughters Emmeline and Aurora (left). Aurora, shown leaning on her father's camera case, also gave her name to a postcard series. You can often find Aurora in some of the Hastings postcards and possibly Mrs Broderick and Emmeline as well. The family lived at Ryde, Isle of Wight, and their house was also called 'Aurora'. This was taken about 1910, at an unknown location.

THE WHITE ROCK INFIRMARY (now replaced by the White Rock Theatre) opened in 1886. It had the advanced design which incorporated circular wards (seen at each end). This 1886 building was actually a rebuild of an earlier infirmary built in 1838. (Broderick, 1905)

INSIDE ONE OF THE CIRCULAR WARDS. The atmosphere seems clean, disciplined and very healthy.

SOLDIERS STATIONED IN HASTINGS during the First World War pictured with local friends. The chalked message appears to say '2/d Surrey Band Boys from Royal Mews Hastings'.

THE BEACHES REMAINED OPEN during the First World War and the beach photographer continued his work. On the back of this postcard are the words: 'Behind is a torpedoed ship, towed into shallow waters for repair.' (July 1918)

THIS TANK WAS SENT TO HASTINGS in July 1918 to collect money for the War Weapons Fund. Tanks were first used by the British army in 1917. This is a Mark III, standing on the sea front opposite St Mary-in-the-Castle church.

A WIDER VIEW OF THE ENLARGEMENT on p. 57. It includes the town's great talking point of 1919 – the washed-up German submarine. It had broken loose while being towed to France as one of the spoils of war.

A PHOTOGRAPH OF THE SEA FRONT taken in the 1920s showing the Boer War memorial near the pier.

THE EARL OF CAVAN UNVEILING THE WAR MEMORIAL in Alexandra Park on 19 March 1922. The sculptor and designer, Miss Margaret Winser of Tenterden, was a pupil of the famous French sculptor Rodin.

THE LOCAL CAST AND PRODUCTION TEAM of *The Norman Conquest*, produced at Falaise and Caen in Normandy in June 1931. Who could fail to recognize the gentleman playing William? The visage under the shining helmet (fourth from right) is, of course, that of the borough's then publicity officer – the redoubtable W.H. Dyer. In front of him (third row) is Maud Tyler, the highly individualistic local Quaker. She is wearing a shirt and tie and wrote the dialogue and lyrics. George H. Child was the producer. Music was by Florence Aylward. Well done!

FOUNDATION STONE PHOTOGRAPHS, although often dull to look at, obviously have one redeeming feature. They are easy to date. But this example (28 February 1931) is actually more interesting than might be supposed. The lady wielding the trowel is Lady Willingdon. To judge from the mortar still adhering to it, she had used it with the vigour that was said to be characteristic of all her activities. The half grown wall before her is part of the brick 'skin' to the Durbar Hall in the Hastings Museum (John's Place). This hall, which is still to be seen, has a finely carved interior, from India, of a kind possessed by Queen Victoria at Osborne. It was bought in 1887 from the Indian and Colonial Exhibition, in London, by Lady Willingdon's father (Lord Brassey). He had it erected behind his London house in Park Lane as a private museum for his first wife, Annie. (She was an insatiable collector of curios on their famous yacht voyages.) It was eventually given to Hastings by the family and transported here because of the Hastings connection with Lord Brassey. Mayor Ormerod (left) is positively grinning with civic pride as the official recipient of this extraordinary gift. Next to him is Lord Willingdon, the very picture of an amiable but aloof aristocrat. But it is Lady Willingdon who so vividly marks the occasion. She was the 'baby' of 1876 in her mother's best selling book *Around the World in the Yacht Sunbeam* and, rightfully, 'steals' the picture.

LORD BRASSEY IS INAUGURATED as Lord Warden of the Cinque Ports at Dover Castle in 1910. As a notable sailor he was a popular Lord Warden, but never lost his interest in Hastings. His second wife, Sybil, is on his right, with the parasol.

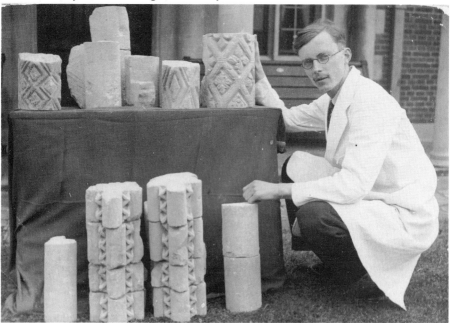

THIS YOUNG MAN IS JOHN MANWARING BAINES, curator of the Hastings Museum in 1937, showing carved stones from the Augustinian Priory – found when the Ritz cinema was built in Cambridge Road. The ruins of the priory are still under the later development – Sainsbury's supermarket.

BOHEMIA HOUSE (built about 1830), now the site of the Civic Centre. Only the walled garden remains and an ice-house. A fake Roman bath can be found elsewhere in the woods. (J.M. Baines, 1950)

BOHEMIA FARM. The last of the farm buildings opposite what is now the Summerfields Sports Centre. The rock garden close by is made from the filled in farm ponds. Undated, this faded photograph was probably taken about 1910.

WHITE ROCK GARDENS, 1927. The Victorian bandstand had by this time been moved up from the sea front, attracting even larger crowds. Only the older generation of ladies has sunshades, and the 'no-hat brigade' (as the elderly dubbed it) is by now recruiting many more young men.

THE NEWLY OPENED BOWLING GREENS IN WHITE ROCK GARDENS, 1927. This has been the setting for many exciting tournaments ever since – enjoyed by spectators if they know the rules.

WHY DID THE MAYOR, COUNCILLOR E.M. FORD, CHOOSE TO STAND ON A TABLE to proclaim the accession of Edward VIII on 22 January 1936? Was the town hall balcony (the usual place) temporarily unsafe?

THE NEW AND RATHER HEAVIER MAYOR, Arthur Blackman, has wisely not risked standing on a table for the proclamation of George VI on 12 December 1936. But why isn't he wearing his hat? Spot the trumpet at rest.

APART FROM INEVITABLE ALTERATIONS, this long familiar corner of Victorian Hastings will be familiar for many more years in Claremont. This 1930s photograph shows (left to right) Dunk's Auction Rooms, the Brassey Institute (the public library), and Parson's Printing Works. The print workers are taking a break on the pavement and often did so. But what has caught their attention? Or did the photographer ask all these people to, 'Look away, please, from the camera,' to improve the composition?

THE FIRST HASTINGS MOBILE LIBRARY outside the Brassey Institute in 1937. Driver Tommy Marsh later served in the Second World War as a Desert Rat. He returned to driving the van after the war.

INSIDE THE MOBILE LIBRARY. Most books were heavily bound. Only girls with stamina could survive in this job. The strong assistant here is Beryl Winter.

THE ATS (Auxiliary Territorial Service) parading at Verulam Place, 23 April 1939 – St George's Day. They are not yet in uniform. Mary Parker is the officer with the armband.

AN AMATEUR SNAPSHOT taken on the same day of the St John Ambulance Parade, outside the White Rock Pavilion, with Idina, Countess Brassey. The countess was a well-known supporter of the Brigade.

ANOTHER SHOT of that 1939 parade on St George's Day. The ladies processing along the sea front are trainee air-raid wardens and were jeered at by some of the bystanders.

THE AFS (Auxiliary Fire Service) on the same parade. These handsome machines, together with their gallant crews, were later to be the saviours in many a local bombing raid.

A TOUCHING SOMBRE PICTURE of sea cadets about to take part in the parade, near the Fishmarket.

THESE SCHOOLCHILDREN ARE WAITING AT HASTINGS STATION to be evacuated to Hertfordshire and Bedfordshire. Not long afterwards, the first bombs fell on the town – on 26 July 1940.

THE MAYOR OF HASTINGS, Dr W.E. Jameson, visiting a Bofors AA (Anti-Aircraft) battery in 1943. These were a defence against the daytime 'tip and run' air-raids. Sites included the East and West Hills, and the sea front.

LEWCOCKS RESTAURANT was destroyed in 1943. It was on the corner of Denmark Place and has been rebuilt in the last few years as Homedane House flats.

THE ALBANY HOTEL IN ROBERTSON TERRACE, bombed in 1943. Many military personnel billeted here were killed. Rebuilt as the Albany Court flats.

CASTLE STREET, the Denmark Arms in 1943. This section of the street was later completely rebuilt and is now being altered again with a pedestrian subway. On the north side (under the castle) you can still see early nineteenth-century architecture.

VOLUNTEER FIRST AID POST WORKERS AT CARLISLE PARADE in 1942. The post was sited in the underground car park and could provide gas decontamination facilities. The medical staff (centre) are Dr G.R. Bruce (Medical Officer of Health), Dr Dorothea Blunt and Nurse Dixon of the St John Ambulance Brigade.

REMOVING THE SEA FRONT DEFENCES at Eversfield Place in 1944. In the original picture you can see the bomb damage at Grand Parade and Marine Court.

GIFT from
HASTINGS
NEW ZEALAND
TO
HASTINGS
ENGLAND

MANY PEOPLE HAVE FORGOTTEN that food rationing did not end until 1954. Here is Miss Joyce Barker of the Hastings WVS (now the WRVS) delivering a New Zealand food parcel to a glad family in Stonefield Road on 8 September 1950. The total gift to the town was 3½ tons – divided into 120 boxes, each containing meat, cheese – and soap!

# SECTION FIVE

# Hastings and St Leonards Piers

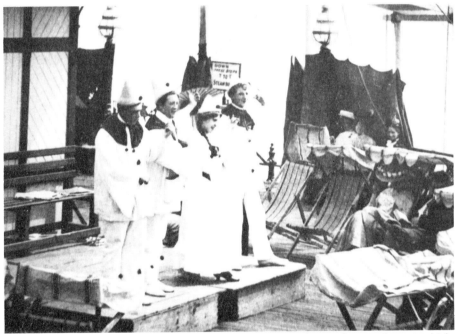

THESE PIERROTS ARE PROBABLY THE WALLIS ARTHUR TROUPE, a form of entertainment which increasingly replaced the traditional ministrels which the Victorians had loved. However, the audience for this show on Hastings Pier seems very sparse and the show itself a little pathetic. The pierrots are playing imaginary musical instruments to some very glum spectators. The inadequate tarpaulin drapes are an effort, it would seem, to conceal the performance from eavesdropping non-payers, but hardly seem necessary. (Louis Levy, 1910)

THIS PHOTOGRAPH OF HASTINGS PIER (built 1872) was taken between 1914, when the bandstand was opened, and July 1917, when the Pier Pavilion (at the far end) burnt down.

A FAMILIAR SIGHT ON HASTINGS PIER for many years, this 1914 bandstand had a 'modern' look which expressed the more progressive attempts (before 1914) to up-date the town. The entry to the pier (behind, right) shows how it looked before reconstruction in the 1920s as an Art Deco facade.

ST MARGARET'S ROAD, 15 July 1917. A little group of spectators, with two ladies eagerly hurrying to join it, is peering between the houses to gaze at Hastings Pier on fire. Soldiers had attended a concert there the day before and one of their cigarette ends was thought to be responsible.

THIS IS WHAT THE INTERIOR OF THE PIER PAVILION looked like before the blaze – an eastern-style design of some magnificence which contrasts very quaintly with the plain (and very hard) chairs.

STANDING ON THE SEA FRONT, these visitors and residents of the 1920s are listening to the pier band without paying – a seaside custom which had always dented the deck-chair profits.

ANOTHER FREE ENTERTAINMENT was watching fires – if you could find one. Here, the Grand Hotel (opposite the pier and now Waverly Court) is on fire. The photograph dates from the 1920s.

BOROUGH PUBLICITY PHOTOGRAPH, July 1935. Floodlit bathing with crowds watching from the pier was always a big tourist draw – no doubt because the lights emphasized the female form in a mysterious, but effective, way.

BOROUGH PUBLICITY PHOTOGRAPH, July 1935. Although it was summer, one wonders whether this line-up of 'happy bathers' had spent much time in the sea. July can be very cold. These look suspiciously like swimming club volunteers posing as visitors.

THE SHORE-END PAVILION, on Hastings Pier, was converted into this small theatre. The Court Players, a repertory company under Harry Hanson, opened here on 10 October 1932, in Noel Coward's *Hay Fever*.

ALAN GREEN AND HIS BAND in 1936. This happy little pre-war band is remembered with affection by many older residents. They performed in the sea end pavilion.

THIS IS A PARTICULARLY LIVELY PHOTOGRAPHIC STATEMENT about St Leonards Pier. At least one visiting couple (foreground) have come prepared for cold weather and seem awkwardly surprised by the sunshine. The punch-ball (left) and the nameplate machine (right) were typical attractions for so long on piers and railway stations, that even relatively young people can remember them. The father in spats, studying the nameplate machine, is captured with his wife and well-dressed little girl at a moment of utter absorption. Could the friendly but disregarded dog be his? The angler (left), with his back to the fish he presumably hopes to catch, looks wonderfully contented. The faintly stirring flags indicate an important international occasion in the town – or are just adding magic to the seaside atmosphere. (Broderick, 1905)

ST LEONARDS PIER. Unusually, Broderick has chosen to photograph people walking away from him. A band is playing in front of the old Burton Baths (converted into shops). A lady (left) is fussing conscientiously over an invalid, and the attendant is about to raise the protective hood. (Broderick, 1905)

ONE OF THE EVENTS OF THE SOUVENIR NORMAND VISIT of 1903 was this open air concert on St Leonards Pier.

ST LEONARDS PIER IN THE FIRST WORLD WAR. Soldiers were billeted in Hastings before going to the Front and were free, like the public, to make use of the beach, sea front and the pier. There was no such access to either of the two piers in the Second World War (see p.116) because of the expected seaborne invasion. A puzzling point for newcomers studying the town is that older local residents sometimes refer to the St Leonards Pier as the Palace Pier. This is due to the fact that its own management had named the pier 'the American Palace Pier' after roller-skating was introduced in about 1910. (You can clearly see the word 'rink' painted on the roof.)

ST LEONARDS PIER, late 1920s – and by now famous for its angling festivals. In a then male dominated sport, the lady angler is dressed in the typical cloche hat and beads of the period. She looks mischievously pleased with herself. Perhaps she has just had a good catch?

THE LAST PEOPLE TO OWN ST LEONARDS PIER erected this 'modern' facade of metal lathing and plaster in 1935.

AS YOU CAN SEE IN THIS PHOTOGRAPH of the pier by night, the new owners had renamed it the New Palace Pier. What it lacked in style it certainly made up for in vigour and popularity.

A LAST REMINDER of the 1900 interior of the 'old' Palace Pier. It was of 'semi-Moorish style' with elaborate floral cast-iron work.

THE SAME PIER shortly before its final demolition in 1951. It had been 'cut' from the shore as a defence measure in 1940, then set on fire by a Verey light dropped from a plane.

# Burton's St Leonards

THIS 'TUDOR-STYLE' ARCHWAY FORMS PART OF NORTH LODGE, a unique house built by James Burton in 1830. The arch was actually the gateway to the 'new' town of St Leonards which Burton founded in 1828. Rider Haggard, the famous author of *King Solomon's Mines*, lived here for a few years after the First World War. (Broderick, 1905)

COMPARE THIS PHOTOGRAPH with the enlarged section on the preceding page. The scene today has changed little, and even strolling in the road (like the two ladies) is still possible – but not advisable. Over the arch you can see the Burton emblem of an anchor. (Broderick, 1905)

ST. LEONARDS

436.

THE GLIMPSE OF ST JOHN'S CHURCH is the same today (if, like Broderick you stand under the arch), but the nave was rebuilt after its destruction by bombing in the Second World War.

A PROCESSION OF SCHOOLBOYS are passing, on the left, the 'low' terrace built by James Burton – still to be seen. (Broderick, 1905)

ST. LEONARDS PARADE

BURTON'S WESTERN COLONNADE. Like the Eastern Colonnade, just visible on the right, this still exists as perhaps the most memorable characteristic of the St Leonard s sea front. But the original shop fronts for Nos 54, 55 and 56 have gone, while 48 and 49 have modern shop fronts. (Broderick, 1905)

UNDERCLIFF, AND NOS 15-21 MARINA, built by Burton. The entry to the shop colonnade behind the waiting bath-chairs leads out towards Marine Court today. The hats of the four people sitting nearest the camera reveal some interesting class distinctions. (Broderick, 1905)

THE CONQUEROR HOTEL, built in 1830 and now replaced by Marine Court, is visible on the extreme left. Opposite it, and left of Undercliff, is The Star public house which was licensed in 1852 and bombed in 1943. (Broderick, 1905)

A VIEW showing 15-21 Marina with a glimpse of Undercliff behind it. Just left of the horse's head (in its nosebag) is a structure with a balustrade — now a taxi office.

WEST ASCENT. A young working man is giving flowers to a smiling girl in the shade of the Assembly Rooms (now the Masonic Hall). On the opposite corner is Burton's classical West Villa (1830). Is the matronly lady, further up the hill, spying on the couple from outside her front door? Or is she merely fascinated by the camera? (Broderick, 1905)

A CLOSER LOOK BY BRODERICK at the other houses in the previous photograph. A fur-coated lady is entering a house while a street sweeper works in the gutter. What an eye for social contrasts!

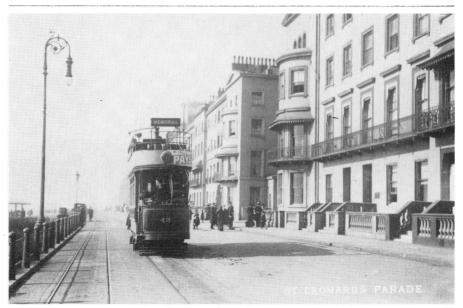

ST LEONARDS PARADE/MARINA. A quiet scene, but a fierce controversy had raged to ensure rails rather than overhead tram wires; the tram service along the sea front was held up for two years because of it. (Broderick, 1907)

BURTON'S WEST VILLA on the right – a house he himself occupied while building St Leonards. It was destroyed in the Second World War. (Broderick, 1905)

THE SOUTH COLONNADE. These purpose-built shops (built 1829) were slightly to the east of where Marine Court now stands. (Broderick, 1905)

MARINA, FROM ST LEONARDS PIER. Behind the beach steps and neatly sandwiched between the fine terraces, is Crown House (No. 57 Marina). Burton built it for himself in 1828. Princess (later Queen) Victoria stayed here in 1834. (Broderick, 1905)

A RARE PHOTOGRAPH taken from St Leonards Pier in about 1935. It shows the dismantling of the James Burton Baths (which had become shops) opposite the Royal Victoria Hotel. Built in 1829 when domestic bathrooms were unknown, they resembled small classical temples with Doric columns. Marine Court had yet to be built (1937), as had the Sun Lounge (1937) now called the Marina Pavilion. The promenade is as yet un-reconstructed. And what an array of bathing-hut styles!

A CLOSER LOOK AT CROWN HOUSE (refer back to p. 125), bomb-blasted and in danger of having to be demolished. This photograph dates from 1945.

A SPLENDID EXAMPLE OF RESTORATION a few years later. The house became the offices of the National Assistance Board – a place of dark brown lino within.

## SECTION SEVEN

# St Leonards-on-Sea

WITH HIS BREAST-POCKET HANDKERCHIEF, gloves, black hat, firmly held sunshade and well-covered knees, this convalescent taking the air at Eversfield Place seems remarkably cautious. Hastings and St Leonards were publicized as health resorts for many years. As late as the 1930s Mr Barry Funnell was still issuing town hall licences for these third-class hackney carriages (as they were officially called).

THE UNVEILING OF QUEEN VICTORIA'S STATUE, Warrior Square, on New Year's Eve 1902. You can still see the bullet hole in her right knee – from an enemy bomber in the Second World War. Before the plinth, hatless, is Freeman Freeman Thomas (later Lord Willingdon), the local MP.

THE ROYAL VICTORIA HOTEL, built by James Burton in 1828 but showing the alterations of 1903. The entrance, formerly behind the hotel, was moved to the front and an extra storey and attics added. (Fred Judge, 1905)

THE MOTORBUS HAS JUST PASSED HASTINGS PIER (right) and the Grand Hotel (left) in this photograph of 1902. Many residents still remember the large but homely shop which is advertised – and which only closed down within the last decade.

THE SAME BUS AT THE FOUNTAIN HOTEL, GROSVENOR GARDENS. The destination board was on the side and reads 'Fishmarket and West Marina'.

CHRIST CHURCH, LONDON ROAD in the early 1900s. The garden on the corner of Silchester Road has gone, but otherwise the viewpoint is easily recognizable. (The Leaning Tower of Pisa effect is a photographic distortion.)

LONDON ROAD, from the sea front. What would Hastings police today make of this apparent traffic confusion? The tram is going *up* the hill on the 'wrong' side of the road, and the carriage is coming *down* it on the 'wrong' side! Solve this mystery with the aid of a magnifying glass. (Broderick, 1905)

A MORE DETAILED STUDY OF A FLOWER SELLER almost opposite the Yorkshire Grey in London Road. Surely this is a most inconvenient pitch if the nearby tram lines are considered? (Broderick, 1905)

GRAND PARADE (between London Road and Warrior Square). A shop assistant is cleaning the window of Lush and Cook's (left), the famous dry cleaning and dyeing firm which started in 1842. (Broderick, 1907)

THE SEA FRONT AT WARRIOR SQUARE, taken from Eversfield Place. Much the same slope to the beach still exists (today leading to 'Bottle Alley'). (Broderick, 1907)

WARRIOR SQUARE, built in the 1860s. Several houses here were destroyed in the Second World War. (Broderick, 1907)

ST LEONARDS PARADE. Did the photographer achieve this view by setting up his tripod on a bastion similar to the one ahead? His daughter stands hand on rail at the second post up. (Broderick, 1907)

THE EDINBURGH HOTEL, WARRIOR SQUARE. The two ladies are taking a child to the beach (bucket and spade are being carried) in the well-controlled middle-class manner of the period. You can stand at the photographer's vantage point today and see these figures in your mind's eye, but the hotel (later the Marlborough) is now closed. (Broderick, 1905)

THE BEACH OPPOSITE WARRIOR SQUARE. Continental-style beach cabins are slowly replacing the old-fashioned bathing machines with the wheels. (Broderick, 1905)

EVERSFIELD PLACE. The sea front was like this before it became a 'double-decker' in the 1930s. An interesting but not a good example of a Broderick. The three bathers on the right make too muddled a shape. (Broderick, 1905)

REMAKING THE 'FRONT LINE' (i.e. the sea front) in April 1927, showing a pile-driver at Warrior Square. A tram noses through the confusion.

EVERSFIELD PLACE in 1935 during the reconstruction into a double-decker promenade. (This was a government-sponsored scheme to relieve unemployment.) The two children have strikingly old-fashioned boots.

THE MINISTER OF TRANSPORT, Leslie Hore-Belisha, after opening the new underground car park on 15 June 1936. He is inspecting the equally new Upper Parade at Eversfield Place with Mayor Ford (top hat). Belisha gave his name to the Belisha beacons at pedestrian crossings.

MARINE COURT with the Sun Lounge in the foreground. Designed to resemble an ocean-going liner, this block of flats aroused fierce local opposition in 1936 when building began. (Look again at p. 127 to judge the comparison with the Burton terrace it replaced.)

THE NEWLY OPENED LOWER PARADE in the 1930s, taken from the top of the slope shown on the photograph on p. 134. A just visible telephone box (centre) is strangely close to possible rough seas.

THE ILLUMINATED PIER AND THE SHINING SAND on a summer evening in 1935 lend some charm to the concrete of Lower Parade. But was it built, as rumour had it, to protect the beach from landings in a future war? (Government money was given to this project.)

HIGH SUMMER ON THE LOWER PARADE BEACH in the 1930s. You could rent your own bit of shingle for your tent in those days. On the left, a lady is about to use a box camera – probably to photograph someone standing in the door of her tent. But what on earth is the lady behind her doing? She appears to have unwrapped something and is displaying it, on the paper, to the owner of the legs we can see jutting out. (Compare this scene with the photographs on p. 137 which show roughly this part of the beach.)

THE ADELPHI HOTEL, Warrior Square in the 1930s, with a very expensive motor car at the kerb. General Gordon owned No. 41 before he left for the Sudan and his death at Khartoum in 1885, but the name 'Warrior' is not a military derivation – it comes from the name for 'warehouse'.

A MILITARY BAND is playing in the lower gardens of Warrior Square on 23 April 1939.

WARRIOR SQUARE in about 1910. Edwardian naval volunteers line up for inspection on Empire Day.

THE TERM 'DAD'S ARMY' to describe the Home Guard was popularized by a television series of the same name. Here, they are parading at Warrior Square on 23 April 1939, when they were known as the LDV (Local Defence Volunteers).

ROYAL TERRACE, 23 June 1947. An ironic and perhaps sinister photograph of the Elite Cinema on fire. The film to be shown was *Blaze at Noon,* and the cinema caught fire at exactly that time – fortunately when the auditorium was empty. The building itself had an 'elite' history. It opened in 1879 as the Warrior Square Opera House, but was ceremoniously renamed 'The Royal Court Hall' by the then Prince of Wales after he had attended a concert. The young Winston Churchill gave a talk there on 12 March 1901 about his adventures in the South African war, and it saw the performances of many musical celebrities. It was first converted into a cinema in 1921 but was bombed in the Second World War. The 1947 fire followed after its painstaking renovation. The cause of this strange fire was never discovered and the site is now replaced by the Royal Terrace flats. These were opened in 1986 by the Duchess of Kent.

MARINA, about 1935, with bath-chairs still plying for hire. The terrace (right) is by late Victorian builders, including Decimus Burton.

A HAPPY VIEW OF THE ST LEONARDS BATHING POOL in the 1930s. Publicized as Europe's finest and built to Olympic standards, it was also a paradise for children, with two shallow ends and a water slide. It also had a private beach attached to it. The decay and demolition has been sad to behold.

THE LAST WORD IN BEACHWEAR (comparing it with 'period' bathing costumes) is being shown in this 1930s fashion parade at the St Leonards Bathing Pool.

THE ENTIRE POOL was a lively centre of entertainment in the 1930s. In winter, there was energetic roller-skating – like this – around the pool's upper deck. Other sports included table tennis, squash and fencing.

EVERSFIELD CHEST HOSPITAL on the cliffs at West Hill. The town was a popular resort for people with chest ailments. (Broderick, 1905)

MORETON HOUSE, Boscobel Road, in the early 1900s when it was the home of Sir William Rushout Bt. Magnification reveals a beautifully glossy carriage with his crest on the door and an interior lined with velvet.

TOWER ROAD WEST at the corner with London Road. The posed trio of locals includes a shrimper. He is unlikely to have lived in so respectable a road and was probably on his way down to the sea from 'humbler' dwellings in Silverhill when Broderick persuaded him to stand still. (Broderick, 1905)

TOWER ROAD WEST. Was this an example of the photographer's sense of humour? The dog nuisance is still with us. (Broderick, 1905)

A PEACEFUL SCENE IN BOHEMIA ROAD on a hot afternoon – with two policemen posing for Mr Broderick in the doorway to the police station on the corner. (Broderick, 1905)

SHORNDEN VILLAS, built here in Bohemia Road in the 1860s, was named after Shornden Woods – a local name dating back to 1285. (Broderick, 1905)

IS THE NONCHALANT ERRAND BOY AT THE LAMP-POST (outside No. 22 Springfield Road) really an errand boy? His cap and Eton collar suggest a schoolboy from the nearby St John's Choir School, yet the basket suggests otherwise. (Broderick, 1905)

NEWGATE ROAD, named after the old Newgate Woods at the top of Alexandra Park, a name dating from Tudor times. (Broderick, 1905)

# Hollington and Silverhill

HOLLINGTON CHILDREN (with mother in an amazingly decorated hat) return from Hollington church in the wood after gathering firewood. (Broderick, 1905)

HOLLINGTON CHURCH IN THE WOOD. The exact date of this excellent photograph is unknown, but it fittingly represents the appearance of the location for many decades. Legends grew up about its remoteness, but the prosaic reason for the 'isolation' of the church was the expanding settlement around a new turnpike road to Battle (in the mid-nineteenth century). A Victorian church in Battle Road (St John's) was built to serve this increasing population. The old church, once a central place of worship for many farms in the district, then became known simply as 'the church in the wood'. For the Victorians, it became the object of a favourite romantic walk.

THE GROVE, HOLLINGTON PARK. One of the homes of the wealthy Eversfield family. The original medieval house was rebuilt in 1804 and extended in Victorian times. The house faced east and no longer exists, the site being occupied by The Grove School.

BATTLE ROAD, 1904. The conductor of an unusual motorbus (a German Durkopp, in service here for only a year) is either chatting to his driver or has been posed. They have stopped just ahead of the Royal Albert pub (still existing).

THE SAME VIEW, 1905, looking back to Silverhill. Motorbuses were quickly ousted by the competitive trams. Almost next door to the entry to Hollington Boys' School is Vigor's, the grocers – still remembered today.

HOLLINGTON SCHOOLCHILDREN at Hastings Station in 1940 are being evacuated to the Midlands. They carry gasmasks in cardboard boxes and are escorted by teachers and 'guiders'.

FIELD MARSHAL MONTGOMERY made a secret 1944 visit to this area before D-Day. Here, he is being welcomed by Mayor Chambers at the entrance to the borough (the walls being those of Beauport Park). Who allowed this amateur snapshot to be taken?

DUKE ROAD. In the centre of the group approaching the camera is the tall and dignified Mr Smith, a water turncock. The quite dapper small boy is imitating a grown-up walk – with his own stick. (Broderick, 1905)

OBAN ROAD, 1910. The heavily-seated ironmonger ('Old Fatty' to the local boys) is Mr Frank Constable. The postman on the step, beside him, is Mr Waters. The man to the right is possibly a familiar local customer, and the one walking away, with the sack, is probably the owner of the waiting paraffin cart – which displays the name 'Foster'.

SEDLESCOMBE ROAD NORTH in the 1920s. On the left is the post office and next door is a gents' outfitters owned by Mr Fred Judge. You can spot him, hatless, to the left of the pole. But no – this is *not* Fred Judge, the photographer.

SEDLESCOMBE ROAD NORTH, again in the 1920s.

BURRY ROAD. The style of these brick-built villas (here having their finishing touches) is common all over Hastings. Burry was the family name of the Clements family who owned Silverhill Farm. (Broderick, 1905)

ALMA TERRACE, named after the 1854 Battle of the Alma (Crimean War). The fish hawker must have found this a steep push even with empty barrow. (Broderick, 1905)

ALMA VILLAS. This is a very dignified and well-hatted Edwardian lady. (Broderick, 1905)

ALMA VILLAS in 1943. This bombed site has now been rebuilt.

THE END OF AN ERA. Local evacuees at Hastings station in July 1940.

# ACKNOWLEDGEMENTS

For permission to copy photographs: Hastings Borough Council; Hastings Museum and Art Gallery; East Sussex County Library; John Manwaring Baines; Barry Funnell; Ray Gladwish; Mrs A. Mabbett; David Padgham; Leslie Vidler. The cover photograph is reproduced by arrangement with the Hulton Picture Company. Many thanks to all the above for their help in researching the photographs. I have also received much help from David Vivian Haines, and much information from David and Barbara Martin, of the Rape of Hastings Architectural Survey, and from Joe Martin, Hastings RNLI; Brion Purdey, Principal Librarian for Hastings and Rother Area; Brian Scott, Hastings Reference Library; J.W. Sims; Paul Smith, Mayor of Hastings 1989-91; the Lady Mary Soames; Sheila Tester; A.K. (Bill) Vint; Victoria Williams, Curator, Hastings Museum and Art Gallery; and R.E. Brinton of the Isle of Wight Leisure Services, who generously shared his research for his forthcoming book *Broderick's Isle of Wight* (and contributed the photograph on p. 85).